HOUSE OF BRICKS

HOUSE OF BRICKS

Crafting An Unbreakable E-Commerce Empire

Jason Portnoy

©2024 All Rights Reserved. No portion of this book may be reproduced, stored in a retrieval system, or transmitted in any form or by any means- electronic, mechanical, photocopy, recording, scanning, or other-except for brief quotations in critical reviews or articles without the prior permission of the author.

Published by Game Changer Publishing

Paperback ISBN: 978-1-963793-07-9
Hardcover ISBN: 978-1-963793-08-6
Digital: ISBN: 978-1-963793-09-3

www.GameChangerPublishing.com

DEDICATION

First and foremost, to Coco, Ryan, Chloe and Noah – You are my "WHY." I could not do what I do without your unconditional love and support. Being a husband and father is the best and most rewarding "job" I can ever do. I love you!

To my parents, who are my biggest fans and have raised me with values, beliefs, unwavering love, and a confidence that I can do whatever I want.

Finally, to my clients (past and present), there is no book without you. Thank you!

Read This First

Just to say thanks for buying and reading my book, I would like to give you a few free bonus gifts, no strings attached!

To Download Your Free Gifts, Scan the QR Code:

Houseofbricksbook.com/bonus

HOUSE OF BRICKS

Crafting An Unbreakable
E-Commerce Empire

Jason Portnoy

www.GameChangerPublishing.com

Table of Contents

	Introduction	1
Chapter 1	Where Are We—and How Did We Get Here?	9
Chapter 2	The Map	13
Chapter 3	Attracting New Customers	23
Chapter 4	Paid Ads (The Holy Grail): What the Gurus Do Not Tell You	29
Chapter 5	How to Get Them to Spend Just a Little More	47
Chapter 6	Buyer Frequency: Get Them to Come Back and Spend More Often	53
Chapter 7	Customer Service & User Experience Can Make or Break You	61
Chapter 8	Bonus: Black Friday, Cyber Monday & Holiday Season Strategy & Prep	69
Chapter 9	Myths vs. Facts	75
	Conclusion	83

Introduction

Congratulations! I know it's kind of cheesy to start a book this way, but I genuinely mean it. Most people do not take action, so if you're reading this first sentence, it means you're an outlier. That deserves praise.

Before I delve into my story, before I share all the tactics and amazing tips on how to grow your e-commerce business ("e-com" from here on), I want to discuss who this book is for.

Whether you're a beginner just launching your first store or already generating millions of dollars in revenue, either way, I promise you'll find nuggets here that could be worth millions (or additional millions) of dollars. I'm going to show you how to **BUILD** the right way and how to **SCALE** the right way. This book is going to be a game-changer, and I do not say that lightly. After reading this book, you'll want to reread it. You'll want to keep it on your shelf or desk and return to it for reference.

I got my start in this whole online and e-com space because I actually had my own clothing brand. I'm telling you this so you know I didn't just wake up one day, start an agency, and claim to be an expert.

I actually learned (and failed) my way into this with my own money and brand. I've been on the other side of the table and know what it's like to be in the trenches.

When I first started my brand, the e-com world was not what it is now. We primarily focused on wholesale (selling into retail stores). We were in hundreds of stores across North America. We were also one of the first to jump to Shopify back in 2011 (we were on Joomla before that). I've interviewed Harley Finkelstein (president of Shopify), who called me a Shopify "OG."

I'm no rookie to the e-com space, but it was a different time when I started. Navigating the landscape was certainly not as easy as it is today, and books like this did not exist. I did, however, see one trend starting. I saw one platform, one marketing opportunity, that was really about to change everything: Facebook Ads (or now Meta). I'll revert back and forth in this book since I still can't commit to or love the name Meta.

When I first saw this shift, I was already losing passion for my clothing brand. I will spare you the details, but simply put, I was unhappy. I remember one night, my wife looked at me and said: "Look, we're eventually going to have a family. I need you to make a decision. Are you prepared to go deeper with this business, or do you see a different path? We need to make a decision here, and you need to figure it out."

What a woman and partner! She was right. I chose my happiness and my future family. I decided to walk away from a business and start a new venture: a Facebook Ads agency for e-com stores.

Now, I have no idea when you're actually reading this—2024, 2025, or beyond—but regardless of the year, back when I started the agency, Facebook Ads were not well-known. In fact, Facebook Ads were so new that every objection I received was, "How do I know this Facebook advertising even works?" It was such a novel concept, and every business was still focused on SEO. Moreover, business owners usually don't like leaving their comfort zones and adopting new things quickly.

A mom-and-pop store was one of the first clients that reached out to me. They were making around $2,500 a month in sales—not particularly significant. A husband-and-wife team operated out of the basement of their parents' house. They were hesitant about giving it a try, but because they found me through an ad, they saw the potential. Long story short, I took them on as a client, and they grew from $2,500 a month in sales to over $300,000 a month in under 11 months—all profitably. Now, at the time of writing, our agency has managed over $75 million in ad spend and has been directly responsible for generating over $250 million in client revenue.

Now that you know all that, you can appreciate that this book is written from the perspective of someone who has been on both sides of the table. I'm speaking to you as someone who owned an e-com store and as someone who has helped hundreds (and consulted with thousands) of e-com store owners grow theirs.

However, I'm going to make one assumption here: that you actually have a good product. Here's the truth: no matter what we discuss in this book, no tactics or strategies will or can help you if you don't have a product that people want. When I say "want," that doesn't mean your mom loves it and thinks it's great. I'm also not talking about your friends asking for it for free. What it does mean is that people actually want to pay you money for whatever it is you are selling.

There is a crucial component that is frequently—and irresponsibly—overlooked when it comes to teaching how to build a brand, and that is the concept of "Foundations." Everyone wants their unrealistic ROAS (Return On Ad Spend. Remember this acronym; we'll be referring to it frequently)—their 5x, 10x, or whatever it may be. But no one wants to lay the foundational work.

One of our clients was about to shut down their business when COVID-19 struck. Since they were predominantly a retail business and only making around $35,000 a month online, they didn't see the point in continuing when they were missing out on millions because stores were closed. So, they told us they needed to pause all ads and suspend our services. I informed them that it would be a colossal mistake because I recognized we were at a "unicorn moment." We were in a unique position where **attention** was **high**, and the **cost** of advertising was **low**. Attention on these platforms was at an all-time high because everyone was home, off work, glued to their phones, spending all their time on social media, *and* the cost of advertising had dropped significantly because many businesses had pulled back on their advertising budgets. Eventually, they proposed that if we believed so strongly in this opportunity, why not waive our retainer fees and instead take a percentage of sales? We gladly accepted, and guess what? They seized the opportunity and scaled to become a multi-million-dollar brand online, renegotiating their contract with us approximately four times in the first three months.

There is a problem with scaling if you do not have solid foundations. Everyone wants to build skyscrapers, but not everyone is prepared to dig into the dirt to firmly cement the structure. If you build in such a manner, it all eventually comes crumbling down—like a house of cards.

You might be wondering what happened to that brand. Fulfillment became too challenging for them to manage, and their customer service was wildly overwhelmed. They couldn't ship, they didn't have the inventory, and they were selling more than they actually had in stock. As a result, negative comments were flooding their Facebook feed and ads by the hundreds. They simply did not have the right team to manage all of this chaos. We repeatedly warned them that they needed to invest in customer service and implement foundational support immediately. They chose not to listen, and over time, they lost control of profitability, and despite generating millions online, they were losing money.

Think about building your business based on the story of "The Three Little Pigs." You had one pig who decided to build a house of straw, and because he took a shortcut by not building properly, we saw how easily that got blown away. The second pig chose sticks because he was a little smarter and did not completely ignore foundations, but he did the bare minimum. He enjoyed maybe a couple more nights of peaceful sleep than the previous pig, but eventually, the wolf got to him, too. Then there was a pig who invested in building things the right way, so when the wolf came... Well, we all know the ending.

Think of growing your business the same way—by understanding that the foundations matter *a lot*. While this book will be filled with tons of strategies and tactics, I cannot stress enough how much your success will depend on making sure you have the right foundations.

With that established, we're almost ready to finally dive in. Before we do, it will be helpful to clarify exactly how you should read this book. There are two ways:

OPTION 1 (recommended): Read it from start to finish, then go back chapter by chapter and do the work taught inside. Read, and then go implement.

OPTION 2 (Band-Aid solution): The goal of this book is to get you results, so if you know where you need help, where you are lacking, or an area that you need to fix right now, go straight to that chapter. Skip to that part right now, plug the hole, and fix what needs to be fixed. Get yourself some wins, and then go back to the beginning and start there because you're not off the hook. We may have plugged the hole, but now I want you to go back to the start and read, pay attention, and take notes so that we make sure the same problem does not arise again—and prevent any others.

Now that the introduction is out of the way—let's get into the practical side of things. I hope you enjoy this book because I'm super proud of it. I think this is going to help a lot of businesses, and it's about time we started telling the truth about exactly how you can scale your e-com business.

Feel free to reach out if you need anything or have any questions.

Jason Portnoy

PS. This book comes with tons of bonuses for you.

Visit **Houseofbricksbook.com/bonus** or Scan The QR Code.

CHAPTER 1

Where Are We—and How Did We Get Here?

This is a short chapter but an important one. It's based on one fundamental insight: to understand our direction, we must acknowledge our past.

The landscape has changed significantly over the last few years, making it "easy" for e-com businesses to emerge, which explains the proliferation of new stores. In fact, the president of Shopify, Harley Finkelstein, once mentioned that a new Shopify store makes its first sale every 28 seconds.[1] I happen to love this because I am a strong proponent of entrepreneurship. I believe everyone deserves the opportunity to build the life they want, and online platforms have made this increasingly feasible. Whether you have a skill, product, or something you believe the world needs, it's much easier to reach your audience than it's ever been.

---

[1] https://www.shopify.com/ph/blog/entrepreneurship.

The COVID era prompted many to work from home and reevaluate their lives. Questions arose, like, "Do I want to sit in traffic?" "Work 9–5?" "Is office life for me?" This led many to shift to the "gig economy." Freelancers began earning more than they ever did in their full-time jobs, prompting them to leave their jobs and start their own businesses. We experienced a "boom" in e-com, especially because, as mentioned in the introduction, we were at a unicorn moment: Attention was at an all-time high, the cost of ads was very low, and people were ready to buy. The influx of free government money, a desire for new things, and support for small businesses contributed to this trend, making it easier to achieve results with online ads.

Then, as more people caught on, competition increased, with big brands entering the market with their ads and large budgets. While that shift was significant, the biggest change came with Tim Cook (CEO of Apple) and the introduction of iOS 14.5. This update fundamentally altered the landscape for business owners and online advertisers by allowing users to opt out of ad tracking. With widespread concerns about privacy and data collection, it was unsurprising that most people (some say up to 90%) chose to opt out of being tracked.

The unfortunate reality is that your experience on these platforms largely depends on your actions and on the platform's ability to monitor and track you across different websites to provide you with an experience that benefits you. If you dislike skiing, for instance, why would you want skiing-related content on your feed? For advertisers, the inability to track people poses a significant challenge: How can we determine the results of our ads? Consequently, ROAS (Return On Ad

Spend) plummeted. Clients accustomed to seeing 5x returns were suddenly witnessing returns as low as 1x. This unexpected shift caused widespread confusion and panic. Many agencies, including ours, took the responsible step of advising clients to reduce spending until we could navigate these new waters. As we adapted, we realized that not everything had fundamentally changed.

If 50% of your business previously came from ads, and you continued to spend the same amount while your store's revenue remained consistent, we could infer that ads still contributed to half of your revenue. Sometimes, applying common sense is crucial in business. The simplicity of achieving results on Facebook had vanished. The metrics that were once crucial to our strategies were no longer as relevant. We also observed that lacking a solid foundation made it more difficult to weather storms, leaving businesses vulnerable rather than antifragile (thriving amid stress and adversity).

Consider this a brief history lesson. Using this knowledge, I encourage you to apply these insights throughout the entire book. This book aims to prepare you to withstand any storm, to make you antifragile.

CHAPTER 2

The Map

"One day, Alice came to a fork in the road and saw a Cheshire cat in a tree. 'Which road do I take?' she asked. 'Where do you want to go?' was his response. 'I don't know,' Alice answered. 'Then,' said the cat, 'it doesn't matter.'"
– Lewis Carroll, *Alice in Wonderland*

If you don't know where you want to go, you'll never get there since reaching an unknown destination is impossible. Success, goals, "winning," or whatever you wish to call it, must first be defined by you, the business owner. What are you aiming to achieve? What are you building towards? When any client comes to us at the agency or for consulting, coaching, or training, one of our initial questions –is, "What is it that you want? What is the goal?" More often than not, clients try to ask us to define that success metric. The issue is that when you outsource your success, you might think you're delegating it, but in reality, you're *abdicating* it as a business owner. Success is something that you, as a business owner, need to define.

The largest problem stems from comparison. You compare yourself to other e-com stores, or you go on Twitter and read about this person's success story and that person's, but that's not going to serve you. It does you no good to look and then emulate, because their goals may not be your goals. You need context, and on social media, where everyone shows the highlights and screenshots of how well their stores are doing, very few will ever show you the downside and what it took/cost to get to their level.

There's a name for basing your own goals and aims on other people's: it's called mimetic desire. We're starting here because we've had many clients come to us with these kinds of goals, and then the goal keeps changing, which makes it impossible to achieve results. So, you need to be clear on the destination and the KPI (Key Performance Indicators) goals. We had a client come to us whose primary goal was to maximize profitability. That's not a bad goal, but it's hard to scale when you focus on maximizing profitability because acquiring new customers tends to be less profitable than retaining existing customers. Inevitably, acquisition slowed, so they began complaining that they needed to acquire more customers. We said, "Okay, but is the goal to be profitable and maintain this margin, or is the goal to acquire new customers?" Of course, they wanted both, but those are, at times, conflicting goals (at scale and from a paid advertising perspective).

The next mistake I see a lot of e-com store owners make is overcomplicating things. Jay Abraham famously says that there are only three ways to grow a business:

1. **Get more customers.**

2. **Increase your pricing: in e-com, we call this increasing the average order value (AOV) or transaction value.**

3. **Get them to buy more often (buyer frequency).**

We've been led to believe that growth means choosing one of three strategies and committing fully to it. "We need to go all in on acquisition, and then we'll focus on the rest," or "We need to go all in on AOV—let's improve our AOV, and then we'll address everything else."

I'm about to share a secret I've discovered about scaling—are you ready? You don't need to focus all your attention on just one area. In fact, doing so is often a mistake. Instead, you just need to make incremental improvements across the board. If you study some of the greatest investors of all time (I love taking business lessons from successful investors), like Warren Buffett, you'll find he attributes his immense wealth to compounding interest. Einstein called the effects of compounding the Eighth Wonder of the World. We should probably pay attention and apply this philosophy to your store/business. You don't need to be superlative in one area. You just need to get incrementally better across various aspects and let those improvements compound.

I understand that including mathematical examples in a book can be challenging, but in this case, they help make the point especially clear. Consider the chart below and follow along. In the first example, you have 100 customers, and the average order value is $100. They each order from you twice. Your revenue would be $20,000.

Supposing we could improve and increase those three areas by just 10%. Do you see how your sales would be $26,620? That's a 31% increase in your revenue, and all you did was improve by 10%. If you improved by 30% in those areas, you would see a 120% increase in revenue.

EX:	100 customers x	$100 AOV x	2 orders =	$20,000
10% Increase	110 customers x	$110 AOV x	2.2 orders =	$26,620 (+31%)
30% Increase	130 customers x	$130 AOV x	2.6 orders =	$43,940 (+120%)

Now, I know you're reading this and thinking that a 30% improvement across the board is challenging, so let's suppose you focused on just one area and increased the buyer frequency (the number of times they buy from you) by one. Just one additional order. Instead of buying from you two times per year, they purchase three times. That's a 50% increase in your business.

100 Customers x	$100 AOV x	3 orders =	$30,000 (+50%)

By the way, I've created a simple calculator that allows you to input numbers and see all these figures for your business. It's part of the bonuses I'm offering for purchasing and reading this book.

Visit: **Houseofbricksbook.com/bonus**

Why is all this important? You need to understand what you actually want and where you aim to go; then, we can plan and measure what it will take to get there. Genuine, substantial, sustained growth comes from incremental yet compounding improvements, but we cannot improve what we do not know. More importantly, we cannot fix what we do not measure. If the goal is unclear, fuzzy, or unknown, we end up flying blind.

KEY TERMS

The following is a list of some of the metrics every e-com store should know. They're crucial for defining your goals and evaluating your progress toward them:

CPA/CPP	Cost per Acquisition / Cost per Purchase: How much you need to pay (e.g., ad spend) to get a customer.
N-CPA	New Customer Cost per Acquisition.
MER	Marketing Efficiency Ratio: Total sales divided by total marketing spend (does not include agency fees). This also tells you your Blended ROAS (Return on Ad Spend).
LTV	Lifetime Value of a Customer: How much they spend with you over the course of their time being a customer.
CPM	Cost per (1,000) Impressions: This is how you are billed on some ad platforms. Also goes up or down depending on competition.
OPEX	Operating Expense: Cost to run the business (salaries, rent, agency fees, etc.).

Profit Margin	How much you make on a sale (profit-wise).
Cost Per Item	How much each product costs you to produce and ship.
RCR	Repeat Customer Rate: What percentage of orders/revenue come from repeat customers.
AOV	Average Order Value.
CVR	Conversion Rate: Percentage of people who come to your site and make a purchase.
EPC	Earnings Per Click: How much each click to your website makes you, in terms of revenue.
ROAS	Return on Ad Spend: Revenue divided by ad spend.

Those are just a few, and they're super important. You could focus on many numbers, and we'll explore these in more depth later. But without a goal, we cannot determine which one is important to you at any given moment.

THE CUSTOMER JOURNEY

Now that we know where we want to go, we need a map to get there. This map is what we call the customer journey. Here's how it works:

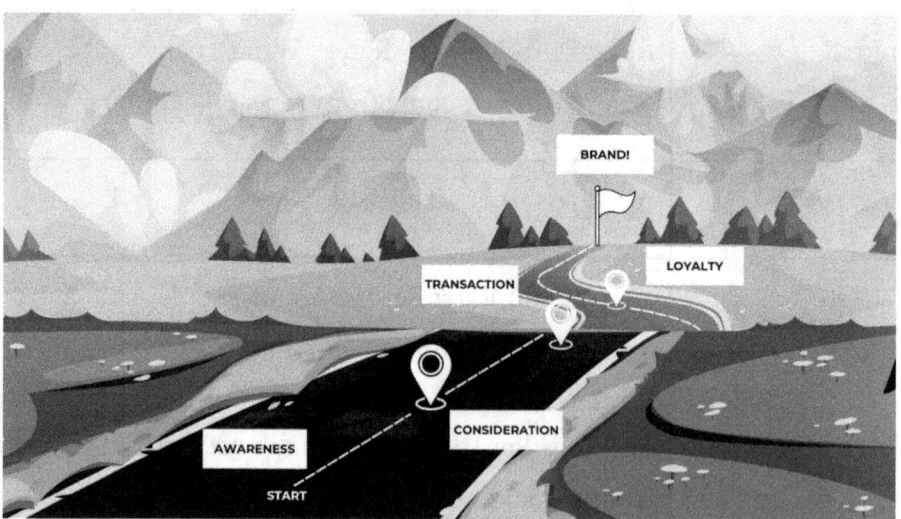

AWARENESS STAGE

The first thing that needs to happen is the customer has to discover you; they need to know you exist. We call this the **Awareness Stage** because we are starting the process of making your target customers aware of your brand.

CONSIDERATION STAGE

The next step on the journey is the **Consideration Stage**. This is when they check out your social media posts, watch your videos, comment on your ads or posts, etc. They are taking the time to engage with you. It may even be that they clicked through an ad and visited your website to see products, read a blog, or download some lead magnet.

TRANSACTION / CONVERSION STAGE

If you do a good job in the consideration stage, you move the customer into the **Transaction (or Conversion) Stage**, and that is when they become a buyer. They make the most important move and give you their money in exchange for your value. Amateurs stop here. They become arrogant enough to believe the work is done, but the real brands know that trust is built and the relationship is established *after* the sale.

We still want to make sure that post-purchase, they are excited about the product and, most importantly, the entire experience with your brand.

Some questions to ask yourself or your team:

- "How is our post-purchase experience?"
- "Are they getting shipping updates and notifications about the product before it arrives?"
- "How is it showing up at their door?"
- "Are they excited when the product comes?"
- "How is our unboxing experience for our customers?"

We have all ordered from stores before where the package was cool and was a fun experience to open, filled with some extra goodies and swag. We show that off on social media and speak highly of those brands.

LOYALTY STAGE

Nail the purchase and post-purchase experience and you will reach a very important stage: the **Loyalty Stage**. Here they become frequent customers and buy from you again and again. Perhaps you even start receiving reviews.

BRAND STAGE

The last stage is where only the best of the best get to. It's a hard one, and that is the **Brand Stage**. They shout your praises to anyone and everyone, but most importantly, your brand becomes part of their identification. When we walk around with our white AirPods in, we are telling the world we support Apple. What do you think when you see someone walking around with a coffee cup and a green straw? Obviously, it's Starbucks. Those achieved "brand" level status.

That is the map. So, now that we know the journey, where we want to go, and what success looks like, this is the map we are going to focus on. Now that we have the map, let's go searching for some treasure.

Again, if you want some of the free tools we give our clients (growth calculator, business success checklist, map analysis, etc.)

Visit: Houseofbricksbook.com/bonus

CHAPTER 3

Attracting New Customers

The cost of advertising is increasing, which means acquiring new customers will become more expensive. It's natural for business owners to think, *Do we really need more customers?* and wonder if they can just rely on their existing customers to keep buying and selling to them over and over again. However, the problem is that the well will eventually run dry, making scaling nearly impossible. There's only so much juice you can squeeze out of an orange. If you want to make orange juice, you will need more than one orange.

Getting new customers is the lifeblood of your business, and bringing them in will allow you to scale, grow, and take your business to new opportunities. Now, there are hundreds of ways to get new customers. (In the previous chapter, I provided a link where you could download one of my lists on how to do that.) You could literally knock on the door of your entire apartment complex and sell your product. We cannot dismiss the old-fashioned methods—the Girl Scouts excel at this, selling a lot of cookies. They don't just give you a QR code and tell you to order online. They knock on your door because they have little kids who are hard to say no to. Just the other day, my wife and I answered the doorbell and were face-to-face with a four- or five-year-old asking us to buy some chocolates. We didn't even ask questions and found ourselves with more chocolate than we knew what to do with.

I would be willing to wager that when you say you have tried "every" way to grow your business, you haven't even scratched the surface. If you are stuck, and your only attempt to grow was trying to make paid ads work (worry not, I have a whole chapter coming up on that topic alone), then I challenge you to really question how badly you want to grow. Relying solely on paid ads is the "lazy man's" method of marketing—I've already shown what happens with lazy growth when you don't have the foundations.

That doesn't mean I dislike paid ads—I run an agency; I love paid ads. They are the fastest way to grow and scale. Just imagine cloning yourself, being in many different locations, showing up even while you are sleeping, and making sales. That is the power of paid ads. Organic marketing is more challenging, but it remains very relevant and important because if your business relies solely on paid ads, you will always be at the mercy of a platform. If the platform experiences another "iOS 14.5" type of setback or undergoes platform and algorithm changes, you will be vulnerable and exposed. To be bulletproof, you need to focus on building a brand, and organic marketing is one of the best ways to achieve that.

Are you posting on social media? It's free. You are one view away from someone really seeing your product and buying it. This happens every day, and brands go viral, but most people just call them lucky and don't even try. To be lucky, you must put yourself in the right place to have the opportunity to get lucky. You can't win the lottery if you don't buy a ticket.

INFLUENCER MARKETING

Aside from organic and paid ads, you could also grow your business with Influencer Marketing. As a preface to this, I want to warn you that consumers are becoming more discerning about this. The best way to describe this is the "Oprah Effect." When Oprah talks about or recommends a product, it makes millions. You don't need Kim Kardashian for this to work. In fact, the problem with Kim Kardashian is that it's now very easy to spot when someone is just pushing a product. The best way to run Influencer Marketing is to ensure you team up with someone who becomes an ambassador or with someone who genuinely believes in and loves the product.

First, do your due diligence. Check their social media stats. Look at their demographics. See where all their followers are coming from. It's more than just looking at their follower count. If they have 2 million followers, it means nothing if they're all from third-world countries that are never going to buy from you—especially when you only sell in North America. We have seen brands learn this the hard way.

We had a client, a bikini brand, who came to us for help. They hired a *Sports Illustrated* swimsuit model to be their influencer and do a photoshoot while also posting for them. Sounds like a great opportunity, right? I remember the meeting where I told them it was a bad idea. My concern was that they did not understand the composition of her follower base. Sure enough, their campaign failed.

How could I have predicted it? They were selling bikinis, and 90% of a swimsuit model's followers are likely to be men (think about it!), who are not the primary buyers of bikinis. Now, you could argue that they might be buying bikinis for their wives or girlfriends. However, that's such a small percentage that it doesn't justify the cost of hiring a *Sports Illustrated* model. Always be sure to check the demographic to ensure that the person you are partnering with has the right audience.

Another crucial point, if you're going to hire an influencer, is to let them handle the creative. There's nothing worse than going after an influencer who knows how to engage their audience and then telling them how to market your product. It becomes inauthentic; their audience can tell, and then they don't buy. Give them full control over the creative, so long as it doesn't damage your brand reputation.

JOINT VENTURES & STRATEGIC PARTNERSHIP

Another frequently overlooked growth opportunity is "Strategic Partnerships." Whenever I'm asked how to grow quickly without having a large list or wanting to spend hundreds of thousands of dollars on ads (and I get asked this a lot), I always suggest Strategic Partnerships or Joint Ventures (JV). Suppose you sell hats; you could team up with someone who sells hoodies or T-shirts. It's not direct competition, but there's definitely overlap and opportunity for both sides. You leverage their audience since they've built a list of customers who share the same demographics and makeup as yours. It's one of the smartest ways to grow, and most e-com brands don't do this enough. You see it all the time in B2B businesses, and I would definitely recommend adopting some of those strategies.

EVENTS

Lastly, consider events. Are you hosting your own events or participating in others'? We had a client who achieved massive success by tapping into the music festival crowd, their target demographic. They attended music festivals and sold their merchandise there. The genius of their strategy lies in the fact that they sell hoodies, and at nighttime, many festival-goers, often dressed in minimal clothing, would start feeling cold. My clients were the only vendors selling hoodies, and they cleaned up! It was pure genius.

Those are just a few different ways to grow your business and acquire new customers. Acquiring new customers is where it all begins: you need to fill the bucket. Now, let's discuss the approach every e-com store focuses on: The truth about Paid Ads.

If you're looking for more strategies, scan the QR Code on the gifts and bonuses page at the beginning of this book and download our comprehensive list of ways you can expand your business.

Visit: **Houseofbricksbook.com/bonus**

CHAPTER 4

Paid Ads (The Holy Grail): What the Gurus Do Not Tell You

"Whoever can spend the most money to acquire a customer, wins."
– Dan Kennedy

This chapter is technically a continuation of the previous one, but the topic of Paid Ads is so dense and crucial for e-com store owners that I felt it deserved its own standalone chapter. More importantly, I want to reveal the truth, the real truth, behind Paid Ads. I'm not referring to what all the "gurus" are telling you: the fancy screenshots or the outdated strategies. I'm going to give you the cold, hard truth about how to make Paid Ads work in your favor and how to achieve success.

My goal is that, after reading this chapter, you no longer feel any need to jump from course to course or buy your fifteenth program on how to run ads. You won't need to purchase outdated products from Paid Ads "specialists." You're going to have a solid foundational approach to growing the business yourself!

I believe Paid Ads are one of the most effective ways to grow a business. I've built several of my own businesses and helped many others do the same, witnessing lives transformed for the better—thanks to Paid Ads. They enable sellers to reach people they could never have reached if Paid Ads didn't exist.

ATTRIBUTION

That said, there are many issues with Paid Ads these days, and even before iOS 14.5, I remember speaking at an event where someone asked me how to solve attribution problems. They were running ads on Google, Facebook, and other platforms and wanted to know exactly where every sale came from. Remember, before iOS 14.5, this was somewhat "easier," but my response was that if you could achieve perfect attribution, it would be a billion-dollar discovery. Nowadays, many software solutions claim they can solve attribution, but that's not entirely accurate. They can perhaps shed a bit more light on certain areas, but true attribution is unsolvable because these platforms report and attribute differently, and they don't play nicely with each other. If one uses "Last Click" as their attribution method for reporting and another counts anyone who clicked in the last seven days and/or viewed an ad, they would all take credit! Google and Facebook also both measure conversions differently. Google also has less data than Facebook since only Facebook has the knowledge that someone *saw* your ad without clicking. It has gotten even worse in recent years. Tracking is a mess, and platforms are using modeled data, meaning they are not 100% accurate.

So, how do we make Paid Ads work? First, we go back to the most important question from the start of this book: What are your goals? We are going to reverse-engineer from there and measure what matters to reach that goal. There are many (and I mean *many*) ways that you could pick and choose a "North Star" for your business and how to measure it, but for now, let's take a closer look at the platforms.

I will walk you through the major ad platforms that will most likely be your main focus.

META

First up is Meta (Facebook, Instagram, Messenger, WhatsApp—the whole Meta platform world). Can we also take a second to acknowledge, again, how the name change was received? I'm not a fan of the name and still prefer to call it Facebook.

The biggest impact of iOS 14.5 was felt by Meta, especially in terms of retargeting, because you now lost the ability to track people across your site based on the actions they took. Previously, you could retarget and serve a specific ad to someone who either viewed a specific product of yours, added it to their cart but did not buy, or even someone who visited your website. You see the power in that, right? Perhaps you remember going online and adding something to your cart, only to be served an ad with that same product later on if you never completed the purchase. The "You left something behind" messages made us think some magic was happening. That magic was skillful media buying. Not anymore! At least not if those people who added items to their cart opted out of being tracked. With the move towards cookie-less websites and data protection, this change is happening across all platforms, but I still believe Meta is the best advertising platform in the world when it comes to generating awareness and reaching a cold audience (people who are potential buyers but have never heard of you before or have not purchased from you in the past). At the time of writing, it remains the best advertising platform in the world (and still growing in daily users).

Now, at the time of writing this, there are different "Objectives" you can use with Meta ads. You can choose to have Meta optimized for getting you Traffic (clicks), Engagement (like video views—people watching your videos), Conversion (encouraging them to take an action on your site such as Add to Cart or Purchase), etc.

When we run ads, 99% of the time, we opt for the Conversion objective. Our goal is to generate sales, so for e-com, the conversion we optimize for is a "Purchase." There's been discussion about "Traffic" ads for garnering as many link clicks to the website as possible, but this often leads to very cheap link clicks and poor quality traffic, which ultimately harms you in the long run. It decreases the conversion rate on your site, negatively impacts your ROAS (Return on Ad Spend), and affects many other important metrics. The main issue is that it adversely influences your optimization within Meta because you're not allowing the "machine" (Meta) to learn about the best type of customers, filling your bucket with low-quality traffic instead.

> **Pro Tip**: What about all the tracking and retargeting issues I mentioned earlier? If you run video ads, you can still retarget those people who watched your video. Despite losing the ability to track people who opted out of being tracked, watching a video is an event that occurs *on* the platform. Since you never left Meta, we can still track it because Meta retains the right to user data on their platform. Therefore, you could run an ad to get a large viewership and then set it up to retarget and show a different ad to people who watched your video. For this reason, my advice is to create ads that are videos, but always make sure that you test different formats (images, videos, etc.).

In the marketing world, the best practitioners know that you should always be testing. Our allocation of the budget for ads on Meta is that 10% goes towards testing creative. The remaining 90% is divided, with at least 60% dedicated to the Top of the Funnel (cold audience) and the remaining 40% split between the Middle and Bottom of the Funnel (a warm and hot audience).

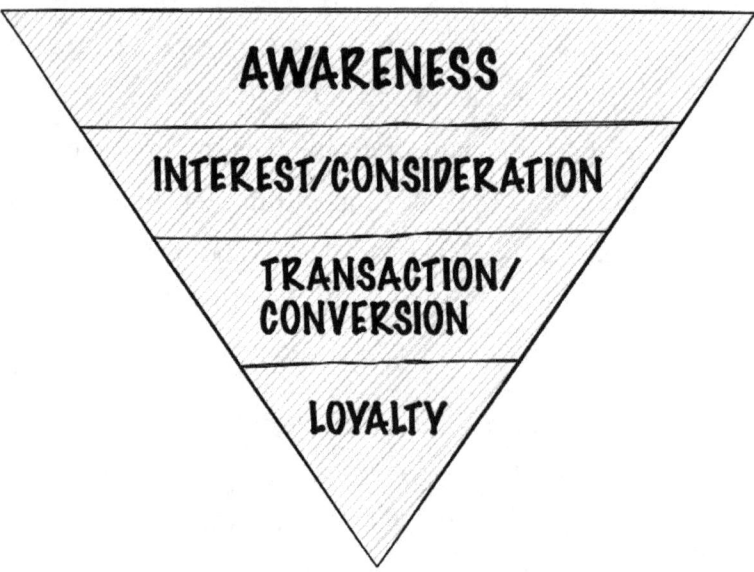

Notice how this funnel lines up with the Customer Journey we talked about earlier?

GOOGLE

This was not a big favorite of mine for e-com (again, depending on the goal), but with Google Shopping and Performance Max, it has improved significantly. However, unless you are in a niche where people are actively seeking you out, it is not the best Top of Funnel approach (where I believe Meta excels). If you think of Meta as "demand generation" (creating awareness and demand for your product), think of Google as "demand recapture."

There are two ways I recommend using Google. First, you have "categorical search"—this is where, for example, someone searches "organic makeup," and then you have to bid to compete with all the organic makeup brands out there for a higher ranking on the page. The more competitive the niche and category, the more it will cost you to advertise and compete. The second is "branded search"—which is, as the name suggests, searching for a brand name. For example, if you type "Nike" into Google, the first thing you will see is a link to Nike via an ad because they are spending money on branded search. You always want to put some money into branded search because your competitors could bid on your name. (Yes, you can bid on your competitors' names, but I'll let you determine your ethical boundaries.) We have seen instances where some clients do not rank for their own brand name because someone else is outbidding them and ranking higher. The highest ROAS in Google will always come from Branded Search because the intent is high; they know who you are and are actively seeking you out. The majority of success from Google ads comes from Branded Search.

> **Pro Tip**: If you are working with an agency (or even running your own ads), always separate Branded Search from Non-Branded and see what is really happening. You don't need to pay an agency to bid on your own name, so make sure they are also working on driving results and traffic from Non-Branded searches.

TIKTOK

Here's a fun one. TikTok was big for many brands around a year ago as an alternative to Facebook.

So, when Facebook was impacted by iOS updates and the platform's reporting became less reliable, everyone started talking about jumping over to TikTok. As time went on, all the bandwagon jumpers who left Facebook for TikTok started to come back. It never lived up to the hype of being the "Facebook ad killer." Advertising on TikTok may be cheaper and drive traffic to your site, but the results/quality do not rival those of Facebook.

Now, I will say that we have some accounts where this is not the case—especially now with the introduction of TikTok Shop. While I am offering you general advice, I highly recommend you test it for yourself. (Although, of course, as marketers and growth strategists know, everything is a test.)

> **Pro Tip**: One observation we've made is that ads (and even organic videos) performing well on TikTok also do great as Instagram and Facebook video/Reel ads. Interestingly, the reverse is not true. Don't just repurpose your Instagram and Facebook ads for TikTok because they (generally speaking) do not perform as well. The reason? It's about how TikTok captures attention with quick snippets.

ALTERNATIVES

There are a couple of other platforms that may be worth trying. Pinterest and Snap (Snapchat), while not as mainstream, are great for brands looking for additional scale beyond the traditional platforms. If you have kids between 13 and 24, chances are you'll see them frequently using Snapchat. That demographic is a sweet spot for many advertisers. The fact that many advertisers overlook these platforms could be your hidden opportunity.

Paid media excels not just in driving highly qualified traffic to your site but also in branding. We have seen clients get approached by wholesale stores looking to carry their brand because they've seen the ads everywhere. We also had a client featured in *Fortune Magazine* after the writer reached out to do a story on the brand, prompted by seeing—wait for it—all the ads for the brand.

Every business is fundamentally in the business of marketing, and advertising on these platforms is the best way to grow and scale.

PAID AD METRICS

Now, let's talk about some important key metrics because, without these, advertising is hard to decipher.

The metric all advertisers love to focus on is ROAS (Return on Ad Spend). It is also the one that causes the most problems with scaling, and most business owners are completely unrealistic with these numbers. When you try to maximize ROAS, you limit your potential for scaling due to the universal Law of Diminishing Returns.

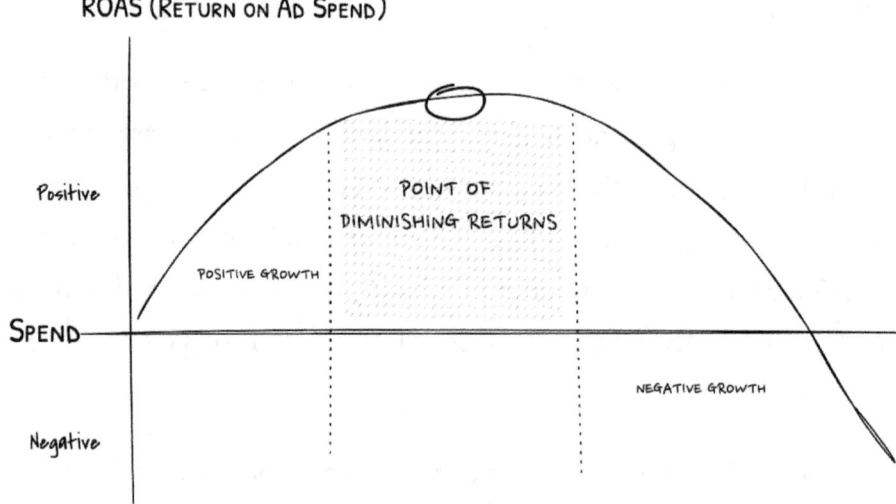

The law suggests that the profits or benefits gained from something will represent a progressively smaller gain as more money, time, or energy is invested in it. The more you spend, the lower your ROAS will go. The wider you cast your net in trying to reach potential customers, the less aware (remember the customer journey) and ready they are to buy from you. Therefore, the best way to scale is not by trying to increase ROAS but by building a business that can thrive on smaller ROAS.

If you are a business owner who is heavily and solely focused on ROAS and CAC or CPA (Customer Acquisition Cost or Cost per Acquisition), you are missing out on the potential to really scale. If you need a 5x return but your competitor is content with a 2x return, they will outspend you and take your market share. Meta operates on a bidding auction platform, meaning the person who is willing to pay the most wins.

One approach we use with many clients is that they simply do not worry about ROAS and CPA. If they are acquiring customers for under a certain amount, they just keep spending. How can they do that? They know their numbers and the LTV (Lifetime Value) of their customers.

For instance, if you paid $100 to acquire a $50 order from a customer, that may seem unfavorable. However, what if that customer buys from you five more times in the next six months and is now worth $300? Now, you paid $100 to acquire a $300 customer. This is how the game is played!

Another crucial component is AOV (Average Order Value). If your AOV is less than $80, you will have a hard time *profitably* acquiring new customers on Meta. As the cost of advertising rises, so does the cost of acquiring new customers. This underscores why the ability to secure repeat customers is so important for LTV. For example, if you could pay $30 to acquire a $10 customer (low AOV) and they buy from you ten more times throughout the year, you essentially pay $30 to acquire a $100 customer.

IN YOUR CONTROL vs. LESS IN YOUR CONTROL

The point is, to succeed with paid ads, you really have to know your numbers. You also need to discern what is within your control (easier to change) versus fighting against things less within your control (harder to change). Your website's conversion rate is very much under your control, but most shop owners do not invest in improvement (split testing, UI/UX enhancements, etc.). It's crucial to remember that the goal of paid ads is to drive qualified traffic to the site, not necessarily to secure sales directly. If someone clicks an ad and lands on a site that is difficult to navigate, or the checkout process is cumbersome, or the advertised product is out of stock, then they cannot make a purchase. The ad did its job by bringing people in, so you cannot blame the ads for not selling your product. The objective of ads is to attract qualified buyers who are ready to use their credit card, but if they encounter a poor experience or a dysfunctional store, you're likely to lose that sale, and that's not the fault of your ads.

You need to focus on and improve what is within your control because if you're going to pay more to bring someone into your funnel, you better ensure you have a way to recoup that investment. To be profitable with ads, you can either decrease your cost per acquisition (less within your control), *or* you can increase the average order value (more within your control—I will show you how later). Even if you aim to lower your cost per acquisition, that breaks down into factors that are within your control versus those outside of it.

Cost per acquisition is determined by your Cost per Click (CPC) and the conversion rate on your site. You can work to lower your CPC, which is somewhat harder, or you can improve your website to convert more effectively (more within your control). One of the simplest ways to achieve this is by creating landing pages. If your website's conversion rate is low, try isolating your best-selling product, a collection, or special offers and create a dedicated landing page for them. This approach minimizes distractions and doesn't link to other items or your main site. We have found this strategy to be effective for many clients, including one in particular who saw their conversion rate increase from 0.6% on their website to 3.2% on their landing page once it was set up. Then, begin split-testing (trying different, small variations of your site until you find the one that converts the best).

Even lowering your cost of goods can make you more profitable and is easier than fixing platform issues. How many people reading this right now have approached their vendors to renegotiate terms? For example, instead of $4 a T-shirt, they negotiated it down to $3, meaning that $1 saved on each order could significantly increase their profitability on ads.

What about your operating costs? I've observed a lot of bloated operating expenses, such as salaries, rent, software, etc.

I know, I know, this section is supposed to be about paid ads, but the reality is that all these factors contribute to the success of paid advertising. These elements allow you to succeed in paid advertising. Paid ads essentially become a game of leveraging what is within your control versus what is outside your control.

I know you probably came here looking for some secret strategy on how to grow. From the start, I promised to be real with you and show you the authentic way to grow your business. I said I would give you tools to strengthen your foundations so your business can weather any storm," and this is the way.

Other things within your control? Consider Copy and Creative! With data protection, we are losing the ability to target specific people, so your copy and creative must become the targeting mechanism. For example, Meta has stated that 56% of their auction is determined by the creative (the image, the video, the copy, etc.),[2] and that creative fatigue (seeing the same ad over and over) results in a 60% loss in conversion.[3]

This is why we require our clients to provide us with at least three pieces of creative work a week. You need to test as much as possible. You don't need to create 800 different ads—you could use the same ad but switch the copy, headline, or target a new angle. For example, instead of targeting "Mothers" for Valentine's Day, target "Husbands" to buy gifts for their wives for Mother's Day. That's the same ad, just with different copy!

SCALING YOUR ADS

Let's conclude this chapter by discussing how to scale. With paid ads, you have two ways of scaling: *horizontal* and *vertical*.

Horizontal scaling involves adding different audiences, trying a variety of creatives, and experimenting with different targeting options. Essentially, you're casting a wider net.

Vertical scaling occurs when you have an ad that's performing well, so you increase its budget. You should consider raising the budget by 20% every few days for something that is "working" (according to your definition). If nine out of ten ads fail, it's easy to feel like you're losing money unless you effectively scale that one winning ad. Doing so can

---

[2] "Five Keys to Advertising Effectiveness Quantifying the Impact of Advertising on Sales" by Nielsen Catalina Solutions, Aug 2017.

[3] Meta analysis conducted on purchase-optimized campaigns (147,610 accounts, 232 countries, 1/31/2021-2/2/2021).

compensate for the nine unsuccessful ones and then some. The goal is to trim the fat by cutting the losers and consistently scaling the winners.

Scaling brings up an interesting topic: Budget. How much should you be spending on ads? Here's Meta's official stance: You need to be spending enough to achieve 50 conversions per ad set per week. To put that into perspective, if your cost per purchase is $10, you need 50 conversions:

$10 x 50 = $500 over seven days, or $500/week <u>per ad set</u>.

Many people spend too little, and I'd argue it's better to invest more money upfront to test and gather data rather than slowly bleeding it out. This game requires a willingness to invest to run ads successfully. If you think you can spend $500 a month on Meta, target the entire United States, and expect to become a millionaire, then this might not be the right book for you.

These platforms are not suitable for day trading. We cannot monitor them on a daily or hourly basis, making drastic decisions and significant changes. As someone who has managed tens of millions of dollars in ad spend and generated hundreds of millions of dollars for our clients, we view performance through a window of at least three days (now probably closer to a seven-day window due to delayed attribution). These platforms need time to accumulate data, which allows the algorithms to work and provide the insights needed to make informed decisions.

To wrap up the discussion on budget and metrics, the Marketing Efficiency Ratio (MER) is a metric you may want to consider. It represents the percentage of your revenue that you are spending on marketing. If you have an e-com store generating under $50M per year, you should probably allocate anywhere from 20% to 35% of your revenue to reinvest in acquiring new customers. This is known as the year-over-year halo effect. This percentage reflects "Brand Power," and if you find yourself needing to spend more, it could indicate that you have not yet built a recognizable brand. Companies like Apple, Starbucks, and Nike don't need to spend 20% of their revenue on marketing because their brands carry significant weight on their own. The stronger the brand, the lower the percentage you can likely afford to spend.

MER was once considered the "North Star" metric, and it still is by some. However, I believe the real "North Star" is the money in your bank. Regardless of what these platforms report, if you're not making money, you don't have a business. The primary goal of a business is to generate profit. The number one metric you should always focus on is your bank balance. From there, you can reverse-engineer your strategies.

LEVELS OF AWARENESS

Lastly, the type of message you convey in your ads should depend on the level of awareness of your audience. Old-school marketers have identified five levels of awareness:

Unaware: They have never heard of you before, nor do they know they need what you are selling.

Problem Aware: They know they need something but are unsure what options exist.

Solution Aware: They are now researching different options.

Product Aware: They now know about your product and your competitors.

Most Aware: They may have tried other options and are now looking for something different.

You need a completely different message for communicating with someone who is fully aware of you, your product, and their need for it than addressing someone who has never heard of you or even the solution your product offers.

By using the appropriate messaging at the correct stage with the right ad, you'll be well on your way to success.

The right *offer* using the right *channel* to the right *person* = Success!

CHAPTER 5

How to Get Them to Spend Just a Little More

We've just gone in-depth on the first way to grow your business (getting more customers); now, let's talk about the second way: Encouraging your customers to spend more with you. In the e-com world, we refer to this as increasing your Average Order Value (AOV).

PRICING

I'm going to list a few strategies for achieving this, but the simplest and most straightforward method is to just raise your prices. Observing the global economic landscape, you'll likely notice that prices have been increasing. There's a good chance that all your suppliers have been raising prices on you, but have you adjusted your prices to reflect those increases? If margins are decreasing because suppliers are squeezing you, you may need to increase your prices. If you're concerned about customer reaction, that's understandable. We don't want to come across as greedy business owners, but we also need to protect our margins. Most consumers are accustomed to price increases anyway.

As long as the value you offer exceeds the price they're paying, you should be fine.

FREE SHIPPING

Another strategy to encourage your customers to spend more is to strategically use your "Free Shipping" offer and increase the threshold (the amount they need to spend to qualify for free shipping). Through our agency and consulting firm, we've audited numerous stores and found that many of them set their free shipping threshold below their average order value, which means nearly everyone qualifies for free shipping. If you want to condition your customers to gradually spend more, consider what the average order value is and try adding 10%–15% on top of that for your Free Shipping qualifier.

For instance, if your average order value is $100, setting the threshold at $110–$115 could incentivize customers to add one more item to their cart to qualify for free shipping. A word of caution, though: You can't just keep increasing your free shipping threshold as people start spending more. We'd all be frustrated if we purchased a $10,000 handbag only to be charged $500 for shipping. Just ensure you're not offering free shipping indiscriminately.

BUNDLES

I love using bundles to increase AOV, and it plays a significant role in boosting many of our clients' revenues. If you sell basic T-shirts, you can offer a three-pack, a five-pack, or even a seven-day pack (one for every day of the week), with a bigger discount the larger the bundle. If you are advertising bundles instead of individual items, you can then afford to spend more to acquire a customer because the purchase price is higher, which will also help improve your ROAS. So many people are missing this easy opportunity.

UPSELLS & CROSS-SELLS

If your price and AOV are low, making it hard for you to acquire customers profitably, it's usually because you don't have any upsells and/or cross-sells. Upsells occur when, after adding an item to your cart, a notification pops up, prompting you to add more. Supplement brands excel at this. Suppose you were about to buy the medium pack; they might ask if you want to upgrade to the large or extra-large pack at a discount (but for a higher net price). Movie theaters do this all the time with their popcorn and drink sizes (upgrade for $0.50 more), as do places like McDonald's when they ask you to supersize your order. That small upsell across all orders can lead to an increase of hundreds of millions of dollars in revenue.

A cross-sell involves offering a customer a different product. For example, they offer you a hat when you buy jeans, or McDonald's asks if you want fries with your order. The phrase "Would you like fries with that?" has likely added billions to McDonald's revenue. You can also implement your cross-sell on your add-to-cart page or post-purchase. You could even send an email thanking them for their order and offering them an opportunity to buy something different.

ADDITIONAL OFFERS

You can offer a warranty or quality protection for a certain price to help drive up revenue. Electronic products often do this with their extended warranty offers.

JOINT VENTURES & PARTNERSHIPS

A really cool way to add additional revenue is through partnerships. A great example is Snow Teeth Whitening. My buddy Josh Elizetxe, the founder, is a brilliant businessperson and marketer. He focuses on partnerships and constantly asks, "Who else within our domain can we collaborate with to increase revenue without competing directly?"

They are in the teeth-whitening space, so at post-purchase, they had an offer to buy dental insurance. They teamed up with different dental insurance companies and became an affiliate. They don't own the insurance company; they are just making an offer because if you care about your teeth being white, chances are you also want to protect them and buy dental insurance. It's a really interesting way to add more revenue, so start thinking about others operating in your space who are not competitors but with whom you share the same type of customers. These would be the best candidates to team up with.

EXPRESS SHIPPING & INSURANCE

You can also charge for faster shipping methods—"Do you want this to go out in the next 24 hours?"—and charge $3–$5 for priority shipping. You can also offer shipping insurance for $1–$2 so that if their order is lost, they'll get a new one shipped out.

These are some great ways to encourage them to spend more, and if you implement some of them and start incrementally improving these aspects, it has a compounding effect. Very few brands actually leverage any of these strategies, wasting a valuable opportunity.

CHAPTER 6

Buyer Frequency: Get Them to Come Back and Spend More Often

This chapter may be the most important in this book. I know everyone loves talking about getting new customers, but the truth is keeping customers is just as important, if not more so. It's also the part most e-com store owners push to the side. Retention is what allows you to spend more to acquire new customers, and as you'll remember, the person who can spend the most to acquire wins. If acquiring is soaking the sponge, retention is squeezing out all the water (money!). We've had a very dense chapter on paid advertising and acquisition because it's important to always fill the funnel, but this part right here, this chapter, is what will make or break your e-com business. I can't emphasize this enough.

Knowing and improving your repeat customer rate (RCR) and lifetime value (LTV) is the difference between outspending and outliving your competition. A good RCR is over 40%, and a great breakdown would be a 50–50 split on new customers vs. repeat customers. We don't want to go over 50% because we want to ensure we are always bringing in new customers so as not to dry out that sponge. Obviously, there are exceptions. For example, if you sell pregnancy products, customers can only buy from you when pregnant, so the repeat rate may not be high.

Lifetime Value is often discussed but not always understood. The truth is, no one really has a "lifetime" to see the value of a customer. You're not going to do this for 100 years and wait it out for a possible return. So, you will want to look at LTV from a few angles: 60 days, 90 days, and a 12-month period (max). You want to assess the LTV of a customer within those timeframes and act accordingly—that will tell you what you can afford to spend to acquire a customer.

For example, let's say you spent $50 to acquire a customer who, on their first order, spent $40. This would seem like a loss. However, if the LTV of that customer over 60 days is $100, you've doubled your return on acquisition cost. The only way to do that is to get them to buy more often, but so many brands are so focused on acquisition that they forget this part.

Most brands do not spend enough time on email marketing and SMS, the two best ways to increase buyer frequency.

The Following Are Some Strategies on How to Increase Buyer Frequency:

LOYALTY CAMPAIGNS

Number one is "loyalty campaigns." When running paid ads, this would be the lowest part of the funnel. I know I mentioned we do not want to pay to reacquire them, but we do want to always keep in front of customers. This part of the funnel requires the lowest ad spend and budget allocated.

BIRTHDAY ADS

Another example is "Happy Birthday" ads. If you upload your list of buyers onto the platform you are advertising on and then layer on the targeting of people who have a birthday this month, you could send an ad saying: *"On behalf of everyone at [XYZ] Company, we wanted to wish you a very happy birthday. We value you as a customer. Take 15% off your order today with code: [ABCD]."*

THANK YOU

Post-purchase "Thank You" ads, emails, and SMSs also work amazingly well. We saw tremendous success when we sent out a "Thank you" to anyone who bought within the last three days, telling them, *"We appreciate their business. Here's a discount for your next order because we know you are going to love it."*

LAUNCHES

Do you have new product launches and drops? We have audited many brands, and when you look at their site versus three months later, nothing changes. The same banner, look, and products remain—they never introduce anything new. The same products are still on sale or out of stock. You want to create an experience that, when customers come back, looks new to them. If they feel they are returning to the same old thing, looking at the same old stuff, they will not be inclined to buy.

LINE EXTENSIONS

Another way to increase frequency is by exploring line extensions. If you offer only a few SKUs or products, what else can you add to that product line? If you sell hoodies, can you also sell T-shirts? Hats? Can you extend the line a bit?

PROMOTIONS

One of the easiest ways to get repeat customers is through promotions and flash sales. Can you send them special promotions, such as private VIP days? You could segment your buyer list inside your email platforms to VIP customers (for example, people who have ordered a certain amount or spent a certain amount within a specific timeframe) and offer them a private VIP Day or private access to a sale before it goes public.

SUBSCRIPTIONS / MEMBERSHIPS

The most common way to increase LTV (Lifetime Value) and RCR (Repeat Customer Rate) is with "Subscriptions and Memberships." We analyzed a brand that added a membership program where, every month, customers who subscribed would automatically receive a new product. Subscriptions and memberships are the easiest way to maintain high retention because customers have already signed up, made a purchase before, and know what they are getting. If the product is good, they will stick with it for a long time. The supplement industry thrives on subscriptions. Even Amazon offers a discount for subscribing—"Subscribe and Save."

"UNBOXING" EXPERIENCE

We also want to ensure that your "unboxing experience" is memorable. Don't just throw your product in a box and ship it. Remember, your customers are spending their hard-earned money with you. Make the opening and unboxing experience so memorable that they are going to want to talk about it, share it, post it, etc. Do that well, and they will want to do business with you again and again.

> **Pro Tip:** Right after they order, make sure you keep in contact with your customers and get them excited about the product. Many people experience buyer's remorse after purchasing something. Develop ways to ensure that you are keeping them excited and satisfied through email and SMS.

EMAIL & SMS

One of the biggest questions we get regarding email and SMS is whether you should send to the same list on both email *and* SMS. The answer is "*YES!*" It's not your job, as a business owner, to decide how your customers communicate with you. You communicate with your customers the way *they* want to be reached. If you listen carefully, they will tell you. If they are not reading emails, they will end up getting purged, but if they are reading SMS, then they will stay on that list. If they dislike one method, they will unsubscribe. Don't worry—they will have no problem letting you know how, when, and where to talk to them.

VOICEMAIL

This next one I was debating not sharing. It has been a secret that I've only shared on select stages or when speaking to my private mastermind clients: ringless voicemail. You can use a tool like SlyBroadcast (among others, with which I have no affiliation) to upload a recording and send it directly to the voicemail of anyone on your list. Record a message saying, "Hey, Bob, this is Jason—the founder of [XYZ] Company. I just want to say thank you so much for ordering from us. I appreciate you. We're in business because of people like you choosing to do business with us, and I know you have unlimited options, so it means the world to me that you chose us. Thank you."

You could also decide to give a promo code at the end of it, or you could finish with a simple: "If you need anything, please email me at Jason@[XYZ].com." You could create a special email that actually goes to your customer service team. At the end of every day or at the start of every morning, someone from your team downloads the list of all the people who bought from you that day or the previous day, uploads it, and sends that voicemail out. Record once, send often! You can also segment it by "first-time buyers" only, so it doesn't become repetitive for a customer. It's an incredible way to show that you're going above and beyond.

A huge mistake many brands make is to stop at or after the purchase, but the real relationship, the actual transaction, only starts after they've bought from you. This is where the game is won.

> **Bonus Point:** Email health is a real problem for most brands, so I put together a video on ways to ensure your emails get delivered (not in spam), opened, and seen. I didn't want to include it in this chapter because it's very technical, so go check out this video here with a full checklist of what you need.
>
> Visit: **Houseofbricksbook.com/bonus**
>
>

CHAPTER 7

Customer Service & User Experience Can Make or Break You

Make sure you have the right team. Simple, right? You could do everything in this book correctly and neglect just this one area, and it would be devastating to your business. Do not mess up; do not trip on this last leg of the race. This is a brief chapter that will help ensure you see what is coming around the corner. We need to make sure that you have fulfillment and customer service dialed in. We want to ensure that you are always up to date on inventory supply so that you can fulfill the orders you are sending out.

Going back to one of the first client examples I gave in this book, our client was actually wildly successful with ads and getting over a 5x return. The problem is they were losing money. A lot of money. You're probably wondering how this was possible. The ads were getting people to buy, but then they had to refund all those buyers because they never had the inventory correct. They paid to acquire a customer but never had the product to sell them. Just make sure you are always monitoring fulfillment. Ensure customer service is dialed in.

When we talk about customer service, this is what they really need to know.

RETURN POLICY

Make sure you have a refund and return policy clearly outlined on your site. My belief—and this is just mine, so you can take this with a grain of salt—is that there's no reason not to give a refund. Someone is not happy. I would much rather refund them than argue. Protect my reputation and build goodwill. A great example of this was when I ordered a product from a brand, and when it did not arrive as described, they offered to let me keep it and just refunded me the money. They didn't make me ship it back to them or charge a restocking fee of $5. There's no reason for that.

Nowadays, that leaves a sour taste. If you do things correctly in terms of a clearly defined refund policy and return policy, you have the potential to get them to give you another chance later. Maybe it wasn't what they expected or needed in the end, and if you make it difficult for them, you've lost that person for life. They will tell more people about that bad customer service experience than they will about great customer service.

ENGAGE IN COMMENTS

Next, respond to all comments on ads and social media. I know there are offensive and rude people, but you can set filters on your social media so that if people use certain language or vulgarity, it automatically blocks or hides those comments. Some platforms even allow you to upload a negative word list that automatically hides or deletes the comments. Take a look at the next ad you see. You'll often find comments claiming things like they never received their order or posing a legitimate customer service question, and those comments go unanswered. The issue is that if it's an ad and people see these unanswered comments, it undermines trust in your brand for potential new customers. Make sure you respond to everything. Saying things like, "That's awful. I'm sorry, we will fix this for you right away," and just showing that you are handling the situation reassures people that there is a human on the other end of all this.

Another crucial reason to respond is that if you have many negative comments on your ads, you actually put your ad account at risk and could even get lower reach. Ensure you have someone on your team dedicated to monitoring the comments on all the ads you run and on your organic social media. Their job is to respond to comments and to do so quickly.

SURVEYS

Surveys are a great way to gather data. A company called KnoCommerce (again, no affiliation) runs post-purchase surveys. The surveys include questions like *"How did you hear about the brand?" "What made you decide to buy?" "What problem were you trying to solve?"* We take many of these answers with a grain of salt because most people are not entirely honest on surveys. They just try to rush through and click out, or they really do not remember how they heard about you, but you may find some really cool insights within their responses.

When you can hear the voice of the people you are selling to—telling you why they bought or what made them decide to buy—that becomes powerful. It can be used in the copy for your emails, your ads, and other marketing materials because now you are not speaking in the language of the brand but rather in the language of your customers.

USER EXPERIENCE

My last point here is about conversion rate and web experience. At the beginning of this book, I mentioned that if your business has a website that is not converting properly, you face an uphill battle. There are factors within your control and those outside of it. You want to ensure that you're always incrementally trying to improve your conversion rate. Even a small increase from 1% to 1.5% or from 2% to 2.1% can significantly impact your revenue without increasing your ad spend or requiring you to send out more emails. Just some minor tweaks to improve conversions could be worth millions in extra revenue.

You want to make sure the web experience is user-friendly, pages load quickly, navigation is clear, and visitors can find what they're looking for without hassle. Important elements, such as your customer service number, should be easily visible, and your offer should be above the fold. The experience should be seamless. Test for user experience on both computers and mobile devices (phones and tablets).

IN-HOUSE vs. OUTSOURCE

I discussed team management at the start of this chapter, so an important question to address is: When it comes to paid media, advertising, or email marketing, should you outsource? Should you hire an agency, or should you manage it in-house? Now, obviously, my perspective comes with some bias because I run an agency and have a consulting firm, but I understand both sides of this argument, having owned my own brand and hired agencies. So, I have been on both sides of the table. I will share the pros and cons.

The Cons: The cons are that an agency will not live and breathe your brand. It's the truth. Sorry. Most bad agencies lie and make that promise, but let's be real. Agencies have other clients, and no one client is more important than another. They all pay money, some more than others. We appreciate every dollar because it represents trust in us to help them grow their business and give them the freedom to live the life they choose. We don't take that lightly, but we do not live and breathe it like you do. Agencies are not available 24/7; granted, I don't think employees should be available 24/7, but you have a better chance of reaching your own employee than your agency team. A full-time employee can also move more quickly and get things done faster with less red tape than an agency.

The Pros: The pros of hiring an agency are significant. We do not live in a silo. When you have an in-house media buyer, they are just looking at your account and do not have the data of many others nor the ability to see a consistent trend amongst other brands, so they react more blindly. An agency benefits from looking at many clients, understanding the landscape, seeing if there is a problem or trend amongst all accounts, and not reacting emotionally. Good agencies do not make quick decisions that have a negative impact. Really good ones are mostly proactive, not reactive.

The other significant pro is you are not hiring one person; you are hiring a team. When you hire an agency, you have a team of people on your account. Many people look at agency costs and think they are giving it to one person, then do the math to see what they could pay for their own in-house employee. This is false economics. The money you pay an agency gets you access to the skills, insights, and creativity of a whole team and all the synergies between its members.

In the beginning, bringing on an agency may not be worthwhile. But there's a point in development where it starts to make more sense because we just have more scaling capabilities. We've seen major spending across the board. The benefit is that we can give you the lessons we've learned from higher-spending clients, with all the insights on what has worked for them.

So, if you're interested in seeing exactly how it would work if you hired us, what we can do for you, and getting a complete audit of your account, we'd love to chat. We always aim to take on clients for whom we believe we can truly add significant value, and we want to ensure you're the right fit so that call will benefit both of us.

Regardless of how you go about it, always ensure you provide the right customer service and experience. If you do everything right but skip this part, you're going to face significant challenges.

If you're interested in scaling your brand, I highly recommend booking a call with one of our team members using the link below.

Visit: **Houseofbricksbook.com/bonus**

CHAPTER 8

Bonus: Black Friday, Cyber Monday & Holiday Season Strategy & Prep

I could not write a book on how to successfully build, grow, and scale an e-commerce store without discussing the biggest days of the year for brands. So, in this chapter, I share a variety of ways to ensure you are fully prepared and can thrive during this critical time. Over the past decade, I have been involved in numerous Black Friday/Cyber Monday (BFCM) and holiday sales—whether running my own with a clothing brand or through our agency, responsible for generating hundreds of millions of dollars in revenue for our clients, with tens of millions coming just from the BFCM period alone. This experience gave me a great chance to measure, analyze, and test the effectiveness of various strategies at scale from multiple viewpoints.

This chapter will serve as a preparation cheat sheet, offering our best findings to ensure you're ready and understand the nuances that can make or break a successful sale. As a reminder, I suggest you return to this part of the book every year around Q4.

For the full checklist, click the link below as part of the free gifts for you.

Visit: **Houseofbricksbook.com/bonus**

Understand that the BFCM period actually starts months in advance. That's when you should begin building your list for email and SMS. Why? Because we want to ensure that we pay to acquire customers when advertising costs are lower (with yearly highs around BFCM) and build our bank of potential customers for those big days when we can advertise to them for free or at a lower cost (retargeting).

GIVEAWAYS & CONTESTS

Some strategies to achieve this include hosting competitions, giveaways, or even offering early access (VIP) for BFCM sale registration. We seek a method that entices potential customers to opt-in and provide their email and phone number.

A word of caution if you're considering a giveaway: I have seen many brands offer prizes like a car or a vacation that have nothing to do with their brand. This often results in many sign-ups for the prize but not potential customers, ultimately harming your list's health. A better option would be a prize like $250 to spend at your store. Then, once you announce the winner, you could send an email to everyone who participated, saying: *"There are no losers at [XYZ] brand. As a thank you for participating, here is 10% off your next order."*

INVENTORY MANAGEMENT

Make sure your inventory is accurate and fully stocked. As we previously discussed, there are few things worse than having to refund new customers or having them turn away from an offer because they cannot purchase what was advertised. Check quantities and ensure you restock properly in advance (especially your best sellers). Communicate quickly with your team (or your agency—our team is on standby during that period) if anything is close to selling out, as you'll want to halt those ads.

THE OFFER

Regarding your offer, make sure it's straightforward. People see so many offers on a daily basis that cute and clever ones get ignored, leading to many customer service tickets. I'm referring to the "spend this, get this" or "spend [x] get [x] off" type of deals. We generally recommend making a single offer, making it sitewide, and not requiring a promo code to redeem it. Or, if you do require a promo code, ensure that it's clearly indicated on your site. Of all the offers we've run, we see those with a 25% discount or higher work best and grab attention. (Obviously, that high of a discount is rarely needed if you are a high-end luxury brand or rarely go on sale.) Ensure your offer is clearly displayed on ads, emails, texts, and across your site. It should be very easy for customers to understand exactly what the offer is.

Use urgency in your copy when necessary, but do so ethically. Do not claim there is only one hour left when that is not the case.

We have also seen special and limited bundles work very well with our clients during BFCM in the last few years. It becomes interesting for existing customers, boosts your AOV, offers people an alternative, and adds a gifting angle.

Remember to update your messaging for Cyber Monday. Refresh your ads (if necessary), website banners, emails, etc. Even if the offer is the same as Black Friday, changing your messaging is crucial.

An underappreciated topic is not being afraid to extend the sale for as long as it is effective. It may seem unconventional, but we have had BFCM sales running into mid-December. If they are performing well, you are profitable, generating new customers, and there is inventory, don't hesitate to maximize the opportunity. Rule number one with ads is: If it's working, performing well, and making money, minor issues like being off-message or a typo don't matter.

On your website and email automations, remember to turn off your usual onsite offers, check all your existing pop-ups and the banners on your site, edit your email and SMS flows, and turn off anything that is not related to your BFCM offer or change the message/copy.

BACKUP PAYMENTS

Here is a big one we learned in the last couple of years from some clients making this mistake: Make sure your credit card does not fail when it comes to advertising! We have had clients whose ads got shut off during prime sale hours because their credit card payment failed. Go ahead and add a backup card, just in case.

> **Pro Tip**: When it comes to paid ads, a lot of brands turn off their evergreen ads. Do not do that. We have analyzed all our clients over the past few BFCM periods, and the evergreen ads are surprisingly the best-performing ads during the BFCM period. Why would that be? Well, they're usually the nicest and best-performing ones, so people click on them, go to your site, and then the offer is clearly indicated there, so they buy.

COMMUNICATION

If you have the manpower, set up some sort of "emergency" communication. Have a way for your customers to reach you should a code not work or if there's a site outage. There are few things more frustrating than losing hundreds of thousands of dollars because people had an issue purchasing from your site. Prevent any customer service problems by letting customers know it is a busy time period (perhaps shipping may take longer). Maybe have a "pay for faster shipping" option and clearly articulate the shipping deadline before Christmas.

LANDING PAGES

If you have a low website conversion rate, consider trying specific BFCM landing pages. Landing pages usually perform better and have helped brands with low conversion rates.

When it comes to the holiday season, adding gift wrapping as an option for an extra cost is a cool idea.

Use all the above to prepare and execute wisely. Preparation is key when it comes to BFCM success. If you decide you want help carrying out any of this for your BFCM, just book a call with our team, and they will go over a whole audit and demonstration with you, showing you exactly how we can help.

> **Bonus (to the bonus):** If you click the link below, you will be given access to the full checklist to use during BFCM, including email and SMS segments. They've worked wonders for our clients.
>
> Visit: **Houseofbricksbook.com/bonus**
>
>

CHAPTER 9

Myths vs. Facts

I want to dedicate a chapter to quickly debunking or even confirming some common beliefs in the e-com space. If, after reading this, you have anything you want to add or ask, please feel free to reach out (my contact information is provided at the end of the book). I'm eager to hear from you. Feel free to reach out and ask questions. Perhaps there's a myth I can debunk for you.

MYTH: I don't need to focus on marketing.

FACT: Every business, regardless of its nature, is fundamentally in the business of marketing. Marketing is fundamental to the performance of every single business, without exception. You cannot generate sales, attract customers, or drive traffic to your site if your market is unaware of your existence. Between 20% and 30% of your top-line revenue should be reinvested back into marketing (halo effect). Believing you don't need marketing is akin to thinking you can survive without oxygen. If you deprive yourself of it, I assure you, you won't last.

MYTH: I can simply double my ad spend and maintain the same ROAS.

FACT: Wouldn't that be great? Unfortunately, it doesn't work that way. This is one of the most challenging concepts for new e-com store owners (or those new to advertising). They scale up, spending more on ads, but see diminishing returns on ad spend; ROAS declines. This leads to frustration and a desire to return to previous strategies where they were spending less and (seemingly) making more money. However, they were actually earning less than they are now.

This phenomenon is due to the Law of Diminishing Returns (which we discussed in an earlier chapter). As you increase your spending, you gradually move beyond a pool of highly interested and qualified buyers to an audience that is less aware and engaged. Remember the five levels of awareness we discussed earlier? Once you've engaged the most aware customers, you start moving down that scale, making the immediate results less significant. These potential customers require more education, more ad exposure, more interest, more nurturing, and more evidence of trust. They need to be educated about a problem they're experiencing. This doesn't mean they aren't worth advertising to, but we must acknowledge that the yield (profit) begins to decrease, which is why your ROAS starts to decline.

MYTH: I should not invest a lot of money in creatives.

FACT: Partially true. With the tools available today, you don't need to spend a fortune on videos or photoshoots. In fact, simpler videos often perform well. By "simple," I mean just turning your phone camera on yourself and starting to talk or having someone review your product so it appears native to the platform. However, creativity is still crucial. The biggest failure we observe among many brands that hire us is not providing us with enough creative material to test. As I mentioned earlier, Meta has publicly stated that 56% of all auction outcomes can be attributed to the creative. They also highlighted that creative fatigue can negatively impact performance, with a 60% average drop in conversions after four repeated exposures to the same ad or creative. Thus, creative and copy remain paramount. Great ads not only get you conversions but keep your costs down.

MYTH: Paid ads are a sales tool.

FACT: Sorry, but the notion of ads on any platform being primarily a sales tool is misguided. The goal of an ad is to sell the click; that's the essence of advertising. Effective media buying and advertising succeed by attracting highly qualified buyers and customers to your site. If your website has issues, such as being out of stock, slow load times, a confusing checkout process, or exorbitant shipping fees, the failure to convert is not the ad's fault. The ad did its job by bringing them to your site, ready to make a purchase, but then you were out of stock. The creative's job is to stop the scroll and sell the click. After that, it's up to you to present your best self.

MYTH: Always look at your numbers by comparing year-over-year or month-over-month.

FACT: In theory, this approach makes sense, but considering the last several years (2020–2023) as an example, it's not always practical. In 2020, the COVID-19 pandemic led to an e-com boom for reasons we've already discussed, making it difficult to compare 2020 to 2019. In 2021, the introduction of iOS privacy changes affected ads and sales, complicating comparisons to 2020. Then, in 2022, although there was some recovery from iOS changes and increased ad spending, a recession and decline in consumer confidence impacted spending choices, such as choosing between buying $8 tomatoes or a brand's $100 T-shirt. These are not fair comparisons.

If you compare year-over-year, month-to-month, or even the same month in the previous year, ensure it's an apples-to-apples comparison. For instance, if you had a significant sale in May, it wouldn't be fair to compare May to April (the previous month) without considering the context. Was the number of sales/promotions the same this year as last year? Were they at the same time, on the same days, or on the same dates? It's crucial to ensure comparisons are made on a like-for-like basis.

MYTH: I need to be profitable on customer acquisition.

FACT: True…unless it's not. No one enjoys losing money, and being profitable on acquisition is a goal many strive for. However, it's essential to remember that the player who can afford to pay the most to acquire a customer often wins. If you need a 5x return on your ads, but I only need a 1x return (because I understand my backend numbers and the LTV I'll be monetizing), I could afford to outspend and outbid you in the auction.

It's also important to consider cash flow and profitability. Being profitable on acquisition is crucial for many e-com brands because they lack the cash flow to fund future growth. However, if your business is thriving, your focus shouldn't solely be on maximizing ROAS but on how low you can afford to go to acquire a significant number of new customers.

MYTH: ROAS is the "North Star" of metrics for paid ads.

FACT: Maybe—what is your goal? ROAS tends to be a vanity metric for most businesses. They like to brag about their ROAS or compare it with their friends', but again, knowing your goals is important. What do you want? Do you want a cost-effective acquisition? If so, ROAS may not be the main goal, but rather, cost per purchase or cost per acquisition (CPA or CPP) matters more and should be your focus. Or, to get even more specific, you should concentrate on the new customer acquisition cost (N-CPA).

The point is, do not let others define your success and goals. Everyone is so busy looking at what everyone else is doing, trying to copy each other, and when they see someone else post an out-of-context screenshot, they fall into the comparison trap. Be smarter, don't fall for it. Determine what your goals are and reverse-engineer from there.

MYTH: I should avoid Amazon if I care about and want to build a brand.

FACT: A year or two ago, I would have strongly agreed. Now, my view has shifted slightly. It's nearly impossible, if the goal of your brand is to make money, to ignore one of the largest e-com channels in the world.

Now, if your aim is to build a distinct brand, Amazon can indeed pose a challenge because your website might lose out to Amazon's established trust with customers. The buying behavior typically observed is that customers find a product they're interested in and then check if Amazon carries it. If Amazon does, they're likely to purchase it there, even if it's slightly more expensive, because they have Prime or they prefer dealing with Amazon for returns or refunds over a "random" site.

If you do decide to sell on Amazon, you'll want to approach it strategically. Over time, consider building out your catalog a bit differently on your website versus Amazon. You could also do things like include an extended warranty in your Amazon package or offer insurance on your product. When customers click a link to register, *voilà!* You have their details and can communicate with them via email and SMS. The biggest challenge with Amazon is that you don't own the customer data. You can't resell to them or fix issues directly, so the "warranty" approach is a clever workaround.

However, the primary goal of a business is to generate revenue. It would be difficult for me to advise you to ignore Amazon, given its significance as a revenue stream for many brands.

MYTH: If only you had more traffic, your sales would improve significantly.

FACT: Traffic is usually not the problem. Quality traffic is more important than quantity. The issue for most brands is what I call a "leaky bucket." Trying to fill a leaky bucket by pouring in more water only results in the water leaking out. You need to plug those holes first.

Is your website converting effectively? Do you have the right SKUs on your site? The right product? The right messaging? Are your ads functioning as they should? All these elements must be aligned because the more traffic you send to your site, the more those shortcomings will be exposed.

For the majority of you reading this, traffic is not your issue.

MYTH: Your sales and ad performance should be consistent every day.

FACT: We encounter this mindset frequently with clients who contact us saying things like, "Yesterday's sales were low. Fix it." We don't run our business or make significant decisions based on short periods.

We must also consider the broader context of what's happening globally. Business owners often live in a bubble, expecting the world to operate according to their expectations. Is there an ongoing recession? Has a war erupted? In times of war or national crises, people aren't looking to shop; they're likely glued to the news, not visiting your store.

Consider this scenario: if you owned a physical retail store and, let's say, five days out of the week, you had a lineup around the block of people eager to come in and buy. You go home those days exhausted from selling so much because it was non-stop. Now, on the other two days of the week, sales were just "okay." Would you shut down your entire store? Would you throw everything out the window in an attempt to fix everything? Would you scrap it all and go back to the drawing board? No. You would either make small adjustments to those days to become more profitable or try different strategies to increase sales during those days.

You cannot view things from a day-to-day perspective and make drastic changes. It won't work, and it puts you in a constant state of reaction.

Don't get caught up and worry about just one day. If it becomes a trend (three consecutive days at minimum), then we need to focus on it and make some changes.

> **Note**: I address a lot of these issues and more on my Instagram and YouTube: **@JasonPortnoy.** Feel free to reach out to me there if you have any questions.

Conclusion

First off, thank you for making it all the way to this part of the book in a world where most people quit. They start something and never finish, then wonder why they cannot find success or remain stuck or stagnant. Congratulations! You've achieved what many fail to accomplish.

After reading this book, I hope you have gained a better understanding of the e-com landscape and how to profitably build and scale your online store to be antifragile, armed with tried and true methods. My goal was not just to provide motivation (although that's important, too) but to offer a proven formula that works. I hope I've done that, as you now have a map and an idea of how to lay the foundation for a long-lasting business with customers who love you, value your products, and buy from you more often.

I hope I've illuminated the essential parts required to grow a successful e-com store and convinced you not to neglect them. When they seek out books like this, most people are in search of the latest shiny object or strategy. There is no "One Thing"; rather, there is a series of small adjustments that compound. I hope I've persuaded you to become a chess master, thinking five moves ahead in growing your business.

This is just the beginning. Reading and learning are great, but they're useless without some form of action. One of my first mentors told me that reading for the sake of reading, without implementation, is just "intellectual masturbation." Go back and reread the chapters, but this time, implement at least one thing as you go along. Keep this book on your desk so that whenever you get stuck, you know you're not alone and have a reference to come back to.

> I also want to remind you that there are tons of resources and free gifts available to you because you purchased this book.
>
> Visit: **Houseofbricksbook.com/bonus**

Should you ever reach a point where you need tactical implementation, I've got you covered. Whether you need an agency to handle all this for you or some coaching and consulting, we would love to be your growth partner.

For the agency, you could book a call with our team. We are world-class in what we do, and we are always looking for good brands that we can help. You do need to have a proven business first. There is a cost to working with our agency, and I do not want you to spend all your money on agency fees.

We have other options. This book is a great resource to help you get started, and we have a great coaching and consulting program, too. All the different ways to work with us, as well as the free gifts and bonuses, are available at the link provided above.

Cheers to the future success of your store,
– Jason Portnoy

P.S. Please let me know your thoughts after reading this book (even if you hate it, I value your feedback). Keep me up to date on your success. I love hearing the stories, and I love helping people, seeing their growth, and supporting their success. Those success stories just light a bigger fire inside me. It would mean the world to me. Share them with me, or reach out if you have any questions or get stuck along the way.

Here's where you can find me:
Instagram, YouTube & Twitter: **@JasonPortnoy**
Email: jasonp@amplifyconsulting.co

THANK YOU FOR YOUR ATTENTION
& FOR READING MY BOOK!

Here are a few free bonus resources to help you grow and scale your e-com store.

Scan the QR Code Here:

I appreciate your interest in my book and value your feedback as it helps me improve future versions of this book. I would appreciate it if you could leave your invaluable review on Amazon.com with your feedback. Thank you!

www.ingramcontent.com/pod-product-compliance
Lightning Source LLC
Chambersburg PA
CBHW050243010526
44107CB00032B/1389/J